Four jugs, all from Staffordshire, showing the wide range of both shape and decoration that was common. With all of them pink lustre and enamel colours have been used.

LUSTREWARE

Michael Gibson

Shire Publications Ltd

CONTENTS

Printed in Great Britain by C. I. Thomas & Sons (Haverfordwest) Ltd, Press Buildings, Merlins Bridge, Haverfordwest, Dyfed SA61 1XF.

British Library Cataloguing in Publication Data: Gibson, Michael. Lustreware. — (Shire Albums; No. 290). I. Title. II. Series. 738. ISBN 0-7478-0190-8.

ACKNOWLEDGEMENTS
During the writing of my book *Collecting Lustreware* my co-author, Geoffrey Godden, and I consulted well over a hundred individuals, museums and other institutions. Their help for that book has inevitably been reflected in this one, and my thanks to them are again due. However, for this book there must be an additional grateful acknowledgement, for permission to reproduce pictures of some of their lustre-decorated ceramics, to Mr and Mrs J. J. Robinson, to Mr T. V. More (page 24, bottom) and to the late Sir Leslie Joseph (page 29, all three photographs).

Cover: *Square-rigged ships often featured in Sunderland lustre wall plaques. The sucrier is also probably from the north-east of England, but the copper lustre-rimmed spill vases from Staffordshire. Tea bowls identical to those shown have been found impressed* WEDGEWOOD *(with an 'e'), the makers obviously hoping to pass them off as from the prestigious Wedgwood factory.*

Below: *The Churchyard Works, Burslem. In a house adjoining them Josiah Wedgwood was born and the works belonged to the Wedgwood family for several generations. On Josiah's move to Etruria they were taken over by his second cousin, Joseph Wedgwood.*

The swirling floral designs in purple lustre on a pink lustre ground, c.1820, were typical of the work of the Swansea decorators though not always carried out in lustre. Brightly coloured enamels were often used instead. Heights 6½ inches (165 mm) and 5½ inches (140 mm).

THE FIRST LUSTREWARE

Lustreware, pottery with a metallic film over the glaze, was produced in vast quantities in the nineteenth century by the potteries of the United Kingdom. This is the kind with which this book is primarily concerned, but it was not the first form of ceramic decoration to make use of metallic oxide pigments. Far earlier there had been reduced pigment or iridescent lustre which, suspended in the glaze, produced much the same effect on the surface of a pot as a patch of oil floating on a pool of water. It was practised by Iranian potters who, in about 1300, were forced to flee their homeland in the face of a Mongol invasion. Many settled in Spain, taking their craft with them, and from that time a Moorish influence began to be evident in the tin-glazed lustre pottery they produced. It was eventually to influence the development of *maiolica*.

During its heyday this kind of lustreware had been exported to many countries, including the United Kingdom, but during the eighteenth century interest in it waned and

production dwindled. However, towards the end of the nineteenth century, William de Morgan, associate of William Morris and friend of the pre-Raphaelites, was inspired to emulate the almost forgotten art, developing a style very much his own. Others followed his lead and to this day many of the studio potters are carrying on the tradition.

In contrast, during the late eighteenth century English potters had been experimenting to find ways of applying a thin metallic coating over the glaze on their wares to give them both novelty and an extra sparkle and eyecatching brightness. Work on the same lines had been going on on the continent, too, and in the winter of 1788-9 a distinguished German chemist, Martin Heinrich Klaproth, read a paper to the Berlin Academy under the title 'On the Use of Platina in the Decoration of Porcelain'. There is, in the Victoria and Albert Museum in London, a German-made statuette of the Greek god Castor which is partly decorated

3

A fine example of a drabware chestnut basket and stand decorated in silver lustre, the work of Thomas Lakin of Burslem and Stoke, c.1810-17. Both pieces are impressed LAKIN. Dish 11 by 8¼ inches (279 by 210 mm).

in platinum lustre. Although its maker and date are not known for certain, it may well predate platinum lustring in the United Kingdom, but it was in Britain that the idea took hold and was to be fully developed.

During 1846 the *Staffordshire Mercury* published the following letter in its correspondence columns:

'In the notice of the death of Mr John Booth of Well Street, inserted in your last week's paper, it is stated that he was the inventor of lustre for earthenware. I beg to state that this is incorrect as I was the original inventor of lustre, which is recorded in several works on potting, and I first put into practice at Mr Spode's manufactory for Messrs Daniel and Brown ...'

The writer was John Hancock of Etruria, a highly respected decorator of porcelain, and what he wrote is probably true, at least

in respect of the United Kingdom. It is not known whether he was aware of Klaproth's work but certainly both Spode and Wedgwood were among the early experimenters in the field, working at first with silver oxide. Silver itself quickly tarnished and it was platinum, which did not, that eventually made what came to be known as silver lustre possible. It did not become available in sufficient quantities for commercial use until about 1780, but it was not until about 1805 that the lustring technique using platinum was sufficiently far advanced to enable items decorated with it to be put on the market. Hancock's reference to producing lustre at Mr Spode's manufactory meant that at the time to which he was referring he was working as a decorator of Spode wares by an outside contractor, which was a frequent practice.

The east front of the pottery of Enoch Wood and Sons of Burslem.

Above: *Three examples of Staffordshire copper lustre. Though none of them is marked, the jug on the left is of a design usually attributed to John Shorthose of Hanley. The white sprigging on the copper ground is most distinctive. The other jug, from its shape, is probably from Enoch Wood.*

Below: *A close-up of the very fine coloured transfer print on the Enoch Wood jug shown above.*

Simeon Shaw's *History of the Staffordshire Potteries*, which was published in 1829, states that John Hancock, together with William Henning, introduced gold and copper lustring in 1823, and that Henning was responsible for its first production on a commercial scale at Wolfe's factory at Stoke-on-Trent. However, Shaw's accuracy cannot always be relied on and, as will be seen from what follows, there is evidence that it appeared rather earlier than this. It is silver lustre that Hancock is principally known for, but in 1816 he did go to work for Josiah Wedgwood II, so it is very likely that he had a hand in early Wedgwood lustreware, which made use of gold as well as platinum in its decoration.

In 1807 L. W. Dillwyn of the Cambrian Pottery at Swansea advertised wares 'ornamented with an entirely new Gold Lustre'. This is one of the earliest references to the use of pink or copper lustre on a commercial scale — an apparently contradictory statement that needs some explanation. Just as 'silver' lustre is an inexact description of

5

Cups, saucers and a plate with heavy purple-lustre banding and the Cottage Girl transfer print in deep pink. Probably from Baker, Bevin and Irwin of the Glamorgan Pottery, c.1825.

A matching jug and mug with purple-lustre trim, the scene of deer in the reserve being in deep pink surrounded by a blue body, c.1830. This jug design, almost certainly from Staffordshire, was extremely popular and appeared with many different decorative schemes, not all with lustre. Height of jug 5¹/₂ inches (140 mm).

Staffordshire porcelain lustre-decorated cups and saucers. (Centre) A Factory Z pattern, c.1820.

the metal actually used, so the term 'gold' lustre also gives a false impression. The results of using gold are not as one might expect similar to gilding, which needs burnishing afterwards. The deposit of gold in lustring was in a film so thin that the result came out as pink or purple lustre if it was applied over a light-coloured body, the depth and intensity of the colour being dependent on the thickness of the lustre and the colour of the pottery to which it was applied. The darker the pottery the darker the lustre, until a stage was reached where it was no longer pink or purple but of a tone closely resembling copper.

Because John Hancock was prepared to hand on his secrets to others, the use of lustre spread rapidly. The widow of another pioneer of lustre, Thomas Lakin, published one of his recipes in a booklet after her husband's death in 1824, and both sources of information have been of great value to historians of ceramics. Lakin's formula was five parts of powdered gold added to thirty parts of hydrochloric acid and ten parts of nitric acid (the two acids producing a mixture then known as aquaregia), to which was added five per cent of

the weight of gold in tin. The tin gave greater body to the lustre.

The solution of dissolved gold was mixed in turn with balsam (flowers of sulphur), spirits of turpentine and raw linseed oil, and the final mixture applied to the ready-glazed pottery with a brush, known to potters as a 'pencil'. The firing was done in a muffle kiln (one in which the piece to be fired was protected from contamination from smoke and fumes) at a comparatively low temperature, the sulphur absorbing oxygen as it burned away and helping to reduce the gold to its metallic state once more. Lustre was always applied over the glaze as it could not have survived the high temperatures needed for the glazing itself.

Platinum, too, was dissolved in aquaregia and heated together with spirits of tar before being applied to the glazed pottery or porcelain. In this case the tar carbonised during the firing and absorbed the oxygen. Finally there was iron lustre, used mainly in the potteries of north-east England and Scotland. It appeared as a pale orange-yellow film on the glazed surface.

To make an already rather confusing terminology even more so, some writers refer

to all copper lustre as gold lustre. Strictly speaking it is, but then so are pink and purple lustre, also derived from gold. For clarity, in this book only the terms 'pink', 'purple' and 'copper lustre' will be used when referring to lustre derived from gold, and the term 'silver lustre' for that derived from platinum.

Above: A type of decoration used by a number of manufacturers, particularly Davenport. The transfer print is in black on top of an overall pale pink lustre wash. This jug, c.1840, bears the printed mark E. C. & T, standing for Everard, Colclough and Townsend of Longton. Note the swan-neck handle. Height 9 inches (229 mm).

Below: Though the teapot, the milk jug and the sucrier in this photograph are all impressed LEEDS POTTERY on the base, they were actually made by James Wraith Senior around 1910. He was the best-known reproducer of eighteenth- and nineteenth-century Leeds creamware, though the milk jug and sucrier here are not as well done as the teapot. The silver-lustre decoration is on a yellow glaze.

Two silver resist lustre jugs, probably from a set of three, c.1820. The bird design is typical of the Leeds Pottery. Heights 5¼ inches (133 mm) and 7¼ inches (184 mm).

LUSTRE DECORATION

Lustre was applied to ceramics purely for decoration and could be used in countless ways, which at their best produced the most stunning effects. It could be used on its own or applied to point up or highlight mouldings, themselves a form of embellishment, or it could be combined with different-coloured glazes or slips, with brightly coloured enamels or with transfer prints.

An overall covering of lustre was carried out in silver and copper and, to a lesser extent, in pink lustre. Most frequently treated in this way were jugs, teapots, coffee pots, goblets, sucriers and the like, though animal and human figurines were sometimes lustred all over as well. There was a call for wares moulded to resemble the very expensive Georgian silver tea services for those who could not afford the originals, and they remained popular until the much cheaper electroplating replaced traditional Sheffield plate after 1840.

By far the greatest amount of overall lustring was carried out in copper. That is probably why so much of it survives today. Towards the end of the peak period of lustreware production experiments were carried out in which some of the later wares were coated actually with copper rather than gold. However, they lacked the deep, satisfying glow that gold oxide produced and in general the later the date of the jugs the clumsier and heavier they became and the poorer the quality of the lustring. Even copper lustre of the highest quality is, however, probably at its best when it has been used to form a background or framework against which other decoration stands out. Its use when combined with gay enamel colours is especially striking.

RESIST LUSTRING

Resist lustring made use of the same principle as lithographic printing. In lithography a greasy surface repels ink from the parts of a printing plate where it is not wanted. In resist lustring a size, often made from a mixture of sugar and glycerine, was

9

Left: A fine example of a moulded, lustre-decorated jug from the later lustre period which could have come from Staffordshire or from one of the north-eastern potteries, c.1840-50. The enamel-coloured transfer prints are beautifully done. Height 6¹/₂ inches (165 mm).

Right: A coffee pot in rather heavy, opaque porcelain decorated with a strawberry vine design in deep, coppery pink resist lustre. The rim and foot border are dark blue and what appears to be a black blob is a strawberry enamelled in bright red. The shape of the pot is very typical of its period. Height 9 inches (229 mm).

used in the same way to prevent the lustre solution from adhering to parts of a pot surface where it was not wanted.

The design was first outlined very lightly in pencil on the glazed pottery and then this outline was filled in with a coating of size, using a very fine brush. When this was dry, the pot would be dipped in the lustring solution to just below the rim, and the rim dipped separately with the pot upside down.

The central coffee pot of these three is in copper lustre and those flanking it are in silver, c.1820-30. Silver lustre of this kind was made in imitation of Georgian plate for those who could not afford the real thing. Heights 9 inches (229 mm), 9¹/₂ inches (241 mm), 9 inches (229 mm).

A silver lustre mug of c.1820 and two silver lustre vases from c.1850, typically Victorian in shape. The style of decoration on the mug was common to Staffordshire and to Swansea.

When the whole thing was dry the size would be washed away, leaving a lustre coating on the background to the design. Firing then took place and for the first time the design was fully revealed in the colour of the clay from which the pot was made or of a slip or coloured glaze if this had been applied first. The best resist lustre was very fine indeed and perhaps at its most striking when the lustre was applied over a canary-yellow background. Ninety per cent of resist lustring was done in silver.

A pair of Staffordshire jugs with unusually delicate transfer-printed chinoiserie designs with enamel colouring, c.1820. The trim on the left-hand jug and the neck and handle of the right-hand one are in silver lustre. Heights 6¹/₂ inches (165 mm).

11

A jug of Sunderland shape but with unusual decorative style for a north-eastern pottery, c.1820-5. The 'cottage' or 'primitive' lustre decoration is applied over a blue glaze, so that the pink lustre appears purple. Height 6 inches (152 mm).

STENCIL WORK

Stencil work is said to have been introduced by John Davenport very early in the history of lustre. It reversed the effect seen in resist lustring, in that it was the design and not the background that was lustred. A stencil would be cut from paper and applied damp to the surface of the pot, the whole thing then being coated with glue size.

When this was dry the paper pattern was peeled off and the pot dipped as before in the lustring solution. The lustre would this time adhere only to the places from which the pattern had been removed.

Some of the most attractive pieces of lustreware had what were known as reserve panels in various shapes and sizes left on their sides for the application of transfer prints in one or more colours, or for the addition of designs in enamels applied over the glaze.

The best resist lustre is a remarkable product, very finely executed, and with a glitter that nothing else can match. Unfortunately, however, the earliest and generally the best jugs were made in fragile lightweight pottery which cracks and chips easily, so few of them have survived unscathed.

PINK AND PURPLE LUSTRE

Large numbers of jugs, mugs, teawares and so on made in white or cream-coloured pottery were decorated with pink-lustre free-style drawings, the designs carried out with bold brush strokes in what was known as the 'primitive' or 'cottage' style. These names arose from the fact that the scenes depicted were often rural, and their simplicity of technique enabled them to be executed by children, once they had been given an example to follow; child labour was used extensively in the potteries during

A finely potted bowl and goblet in mottle pink lustre, probably from Newcastle, but of a kind made in most of the centres of ceramic manufacture.

12

the nineteenth century. Cottage-style decoration was to be found on the products of most of the many Staffordshire factories and also on those of Sunderland, Newcastle, Swansea, Yorkshire and most of the other potteries, which makes the positive attribution of one of these pieces to a particular area, let alone a particular pottery, extremely difficult.

Sunderland and Newcastle had their own distinctive way of using pink lustre, decorating many of their wares with broad, swirling brush strokes, sometimes using them in conjunction with areas of 'mottled' pink lustre. This latter effect, also known as 'splashed' lustre and used in other pottery centres as well, was achieved by spraying fine drops of oil on to an area of newly applied lustre while it was still wet, so that little pools were formed which would, when the lustre was fired and the oil burned away, leave a mottled surface.

TRANSFER PRINTING

The potteries of the north-east also made great use of transfer printing. These transfers, printed from engraved copper plates on to tissue paper, were applied to the pots over the glaze, and many of those from both Sunderland and Newcastle feature the iron

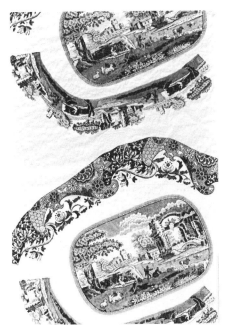

A section from a tissue-paper roll newly printed with a Spode transfer design. The design appears in reverse so that when applied to the piece to be decorated it will come out the right way round.

A set of three porcelain jugs, the necks with the design moulded in rather than sprigged. The painting of these is freehand, but the hunting scenes are coloured transfer prints, c.1830. Heights 5 inches (127 mm), 4½ inches (114 mm) and 4 inches (102 mm). As they are of porcelain a Staffordshire origin is likely but they could be Welsh: no porcelain was produced by the north-eastern potteries.

13

bridge over the river Wear in Sunderland, so that it became almost their trademark. Other designs showed full-rigged sailing ships, masonic symbols or those of the Ancient Order of Oddfellows, and mock heraldry in the form of the farmers' arms, the blacksmiths' arms and so on, while the majority of jugs had on the reverse side a doggerel rhyme contained within a decorative border. 'The Sailor's Farewell' was a great favourite and there were very many more, as often as not with a similar nautical flavour.

Transfer prints from the north-east were generally in black, but other areas often used sepia and rather virulent puce. Sometimes they used more than one colour and, almost without exception, the transfers from pottery centres other than Sunderland and Newcastle were based on prints and magazine and book illustrations by other people and showed little creative inspiration.

BAT PRINTING

A different way of producing multi-coloured transfer prints was developed late in the 1760s, though it was not until about 1820 that the process had been developed sufficiently for commercial use. A flexible sheet of gelatine (a bat) was used to transfer the design in oil from the engraved copper plate to the glazed pottery. Different-coloured pigments in powdered form were then dusted on to the oil before firing. When heated, the oil vaporised and the pigments fused to the glaze. The use of a number of colours, which was one of its advantages, required considerable skill, but bat printing could also be carried out in one colour. It was much used in conjunction with lustre.

SPRIGGING

Sprigging consisted of cast or moulded ornamentation being applied by hand to the surface of a piece of pottery. It is so named because early decoration of this kind often consisted of representations of flowers and leaves.

Sprigging was used extensively on lustreware. Sometimes, if a white clay was used for the sprigging, it was left in its natural colour, producing an effect much like Wedgwood jasper ware but with a lustre

background to the sprigging rather than a blue or green one. Perhaps the most striking examples of this are to be found on jugs usually attributed to the Shorthose Pottery of Staffordshire.

Sprigging was more often enamelled than lustred and decorations consisting of bands of flowers and leaves treated in this way in the brightest colours added greatly to the attractions of copper-lustre jugs and goblets. Sometimes there would be copper lustre on the outside of such a jug and pink lustre inside, while many had wide bands of coloured slip or glaze, over which other decoration could be applied. Another variation was the application of a transfer print of a round white clock face to the sides of jugs and vases from both the Staffordshire and the Welsh potteries. It was said that these would be seen by and impress the neighbours of those not wealthy enough to possess a real clock.

A fine example of a copper lustre jug of the 1820-30 period with a coloured band round a body decorated with sprigging in contrasting colours. Probably Staffordshire, but of a kind much copied elsewhere. Height 6 inches (152 mm).

Bough pots or flower holders came in many shapes and most, like the rather unusual one shown, have now lost their perforated lids. This one has been described as a crocus pot, c.1815-25. Height 5 inches (127 mm).

STAFFORDSHIRE LUSTREWARE MANUFACTURERS

Although porcelain and pottery were made in many places, the area around Stoke-on-Trent in Staffordshire has been known as the Potteries since the time of the industrial revolution after the Napoleonic Wars, though pottery making began there long before that. The Potteries during the early lustre period consisted of Stoke itself and five adjoining towns: Tunstall, Hanley, Burslem, Fenton and Longton, all established centres of pottery manufacture in their own right. It was not until 1910 that the six towns were to combine under the name of Stoke-on-Trent.

No fewer than 250 potteries in the Stoke area are known to have used lustre decoration, either as manufacturers themselves or as decorators for other producers. A very few, with Wedgwood being the prime example, carried on into the twentieth century, but most firms, set up by people who were potters rather than businessmen, had quite a short existence. With bad management, both financial and organisational, bankruptcy was common.

It will have been gathered that the Staffordshire pottery industry was a large one and it had a flourishing export business, at least until more advanced potting techniques for mass production were developed on the continent of Europe and brought competition that it was hard to combat. However, during the first half of the nineteenth century, though the output of the north-eastern potteries of Sunderland and Newcastle and of the Leeds and Swansea factories was very large, it could not match that of Stoke and the other five towns. The Staffordshire manufacturers also tended to set the trend in lustre design and their ideas were freely and accurately copied, with little, if any, acknowledgement. Details of some of the most important manufacturers in the Stoke area follow in alphabetical order.

William Adams and Sons were one of the leading manufacturers of both porcelain and earthenware and probably produced lustre-decorated items from about 1805, so that they were among the first in the field. Invoices from the Adams firm have been

15

An exceptionally handsome lustre-decorated Staffordshire jug, c.1815. The main body is yellow and the figure of the bugler is not a transfer print but hand-painted. The uniform has not been identified with certainty, but it might be that of the Artillery or else the Yeoman Cavalry. Height 8 inches (203 mm).

preserved confirming that it did use lustre decoration, though actual marked items are rare.

The firm of *Allertons* of Longton, on the other hand, marked a lot of its wares with its name and was one of the few to carry on producing large quantities of its not very distinguished lustre-decorated teawares well into the twentieth century.

William Bailey and William Batkin formed the firm of *Bailey and Batkin* in

1814 and an order book of 1816 from an American trader lists gold-lustre coffee pots and teapots with matching sugar bowls and creamers, as well as the same combination in silver lustre. Their most unusual and notable products were their silver-lustred perdifumes, used for air purification. The firm also carried on a thriving business as lustre decorators for other manufacturers.

Davenport of Longton (1844-87) produced a great deal of lustreware of all kinds

Three sucriers of varied design and decoration. The one on the left is of porcelain and could be from the Adams factory, c.1825.

Dogs such as these were made in their thousands in sets of different sizes. They came from most of the ceramic centres, but this pair is a little unusual in that the moulding is highlighted in pink lustre rather than gilt. The smallest dogs would be for chimneypiece ornaments, but the larger ones like those shown, at 13½ inches (343 mm) high, would be placed at either side of the hearth. These date from c.1820 onwards, but they are being reproduced today.

Three cream jugs showing variety in both design and decoration. That on the left is in porcelain and is probably from the Adams factory, c.1825.

between about 1830 and 1850. The firm seemed to favour pink rather than any of the other lustre colours, and often its products were marked with the Davenport name combined with an anchor.

Thomas Lakin of Burslem and Stoke has already been mentioned in the first chapter. He first set up on his own, subsequently went to Davenport, where he may well have acquired his knowledge of lustreware, and certainly extended it, and then went into business on his own again. He produced earthenwares of the highest quality, some impressed with his name, but eventually the business failed and, after a period of decorating wares for others, he went to the Leeds Pottery in 1818.

Many nineteenth-century jug designs were popular, but one was exceptionally so, judging by the numbers of examples that

Teapots of every conceivable shape were decorated in lustre. This example incorporates an attractive coloured transfer print as well. Probably Adams, c.1825.

Part of a child's tea service from 1844 with the impressed name and anchor mark of the Davenport factory.

have survived to this day. This was the Polka jug pattern featuring moulded figures of a pair of dancers, registered by *George Ray* of Hanley in 1852 and copied by countless other potteries in the late nineteenth century, and even in Scotland.

Although lustreware that can be attributed with certainty to the *Spode* factory is a rarity, there is little doubt that a good deal was produced, some of it porcelain. Examples of silver-lustred teaware can be seen in the Spode factory museum in Stoke, and at least some of it was decorated in the Daniel workshops where John Hancock had been employed since 1805.

The lustre-decorated ceramics from the *Wedgwood* factory are probably the best documented of them all, in part because the

Wedgwood was one of the few firms to carry on producing lustreware into the twentieth century. These three jugs are from the 1930-40 period, that on the right being a design in silver lustre by Alfred Powell.

Elements in the design, as well as its fine execution, link this copper-lustre jug to the factory of Enoch Wood, c.1825-35. The front of the jug has an elaborate sprigged moulding of the English rose, the Scottish thistle and the Irish harp. Height 7 inches (178 mm).

factory has been in continuous production from 1759 to the present day and also because so many of its wares were marked with its name. Lustre was produced during the period of Josiah Wedgwood II and was used on a wide range of ceramics. Its variegated lustre appeared on shell-shaped dessert services and its Fairyland lustre was unique.

David Wilson of Hanley (1801-17) took over the family firm on his brother's death and was to produce some of the finest silver and copper lustreware, both in pottery and porcelain, much of it impressed WILSON, and with its design origins clearly in the classical period.

Another important Staffordshire potting family of this time was that of Wood. Enoch Wood stands out for his great potting skill and in 1790 he joined forces with James Caldwell to form the firm of *Wood and Caldwell*, which became one of the largest producers of Staffordshire ware of all kinds, not just of lustre. However, in 1818 Enoch Wood separated from his partner, though he continued in business as *Enoch Wood and Sons* until 1846. They produced a vast range of jugs of all sizes with transfer prints set in coloured reserves or else brightly coloured sprigging on the lustre itself or on wide bands of blue slip.

Factory Z is an unsatisfactory name for a

20

A pair of Staffordshire jugs (above) with finely executed sprigging on blue grounds and each with purple lustre trim, c.1812-15. The jug on the left carries the impressed mark WOOD & CALDWELL (see detail, right) and it is quite likely that the other jug is from the same source, though it could be from Enoch Wood. On it, lustre is used extensively to decorate the sprigging, which is unusual. Heights 4¹/₂ inches (114 mm).

Lustre-decorated dishes, the one in the centre, with its broad purple-lustre border and decorative vine pattern, coming from Factory Z, c.1810. Diameters 8 inches (203 mm).

firm that no one has been able to identify but which had a very large output of New Hall-type wares, often decorated with bat-printed designs in addition to lustre on a bone china body. They are clearly identifiable as coming from one source, but what that source was remains a mystery. Factory Z was in operation from about 1790 to 1820.

Among the producers of lustreware in the twentieth century were the *Wade Group* of potteries at Burslem and, perhaps the most important, the firm founded by *A. E. Gray* of Hanley. Gray was a decorator rather than a potter and used lustre extensively, often on reproductions of nineteenth-century pieces as well as on original designs.

A twentieth-century reproduction of a nineteenth-century jug with mottled lustre and black transfer-print decoration. It is typical of the products of the Staffordshire decorator A. E. Gray.

Pink-lustre and enamel decorated moulded jugs from the period when lustre decoration was on the decline, from about 1860 onwards. The centre jug is based on the Polka design of George Ray of Longton, which was registered in 1852, but the rather crude execution of this sample makes it likely that this is one of the later copies carried out by many other manufacturers. Average heights 8 inches (203 mm).

A selection of Sunderland wall plaques. The transfer print on the one on the left depicts Queen Victoria and Napoleon III of France and celebrates the union of the two countries in 1854. It is impressed DIXON & CO. *The central plaque is a typical example of the many designs that bore short religious texts and probably dates from twenty years earlier.*

OTHER MANUFACTURERS

After its initial development in Staffordshire the use of lustre spread very rapidly to most other centres of pottery manufacture though curiously, in view of its tremendous popularity, it was never adopted by the London potters. The furthest south it reached was the Swansea area of South Wales while, by the 1820s, it was also being used in considerable quantities in Sunderland, Newcastle, Middlesbrough and Stockton in north-east England, in Leeds and some of the other Yorkshire potteries, probably in Liverpool at the Herculaneum factory, and in a number of other places.

SUNDERLAND

There had been potteries around Sunderland since the sixteenth century, so that the industry was well established by the time lustre decoration was introduced. Local clays were there for the taking and Sunderland, being a seaport, was in an ideal position for the export of its wares. It is rather unfortunate, however, that the belief has grown up that all pink lustre comes from Sunderland, for it was used in all the centres of manufacture to a greater or lesser extent, not least in Sunderland's near neighbour, Newcastle. When comparing the output of these two places, however, it can be confusing in that a Newcastle jug may well bear a transfer print of the Sunderland Iron Bridge. This was in part because the Maling family firm moved to Newcastle from Sunderland in 1840, taking their copper plates for transfer printing with them, and in part because, if one pottery went out of business in the area, its plates were likely to be bought by another, either on the Wear or on the Tyne.

Taking the main Sunderland manufacturers in alphabetical order, first comes the *Deptford Pottery*, established by William Ball in 1857. Unlike so many of his contemporaries, he was a first-rate businessman and the company soon became a major force, taking advantage of the newly opened

Until comparatively recently this jug would have been said to typify all Sunderland jugs — a pink or purple lustre trim; pink lustre swirls over the rest of the full, rounded body; the plain, looped handle, and the Wear Bridge transfer print, in this case incorporating the maker's name, DIXON & CO (height 6½ inches or 165 mm, c.1813). Now jugs with flat-topped handles, for long considered an indication of Staffordshire origin, and with blue banding on the bodies, have also been identified as coming from Sunderland.

A very fine Sunderland puzzle jug, c.1820, bearing one of the many Wear Bridge transfer prints. This one incorporates the maker's name, SCOTT & SONS. Height 7 inches (178 mm).

24

Examples of 'cottage style' pink lustre decoration from different areas. The sucrier, in pottery like all Sunderland wares, is probably from the Dawson factory. The dish and saucers, in porcelain, more likely come from Staffordshire.

railway for its supply of white clays from the south. The firm continued under the name of *Ball Brothers* until well into the twentieth century, even though their products were not of the highest quality. They made use of the orange iron lustre more than most and their transfer printing was quite often in colours rather than the traditional Sunderland black.

The *Low Ford* or *Dawson's Pottery* thrived from the time John Dawson founded it around 1790 until his death in 1848, after which, under his grandsons' management, it quickly foundered. During its period of

A Sunderland bowl impressed MOORE & CO with a Wear Bridge transfer print. On the reverse is a second print showing the flags of France and Britain intertwined, which indicates a date after the union of the two countries for the prosecution of the Crimean War in 1854. Diameter 8³/₄ inches (222 mm).

25

prosperity, however, it was one of the largest producers of lustreware in the district and the quality of its wares was amongst the best. When used, marks incorporated the name DAWSON.

William Maling founded the *North Hylton Pottery* in 1762, with John Phillips as manager. In 1815 Maling's son, Robert, transferred the firm to a completely new works, the *Ouseburn Bridge Pottery* in Newcastle. The Phillips family took over the old firm, but it closed down about 1850.

The *Southwick* or *Scott's Pottery* was another dating from the eighteenth century, starting up in 1788 and being managed by succeeding generations of the Scott family with great success for over one hundred years. When it finally failed in 1896, Ball Brothers bought the printing plates as they had done with so many others before. Marks incorporate the name SCOTT.

The *Sunderland* or *'Garrison' Pottery* was one of the most successful of all and was leased to John Phillips, who had been helping to run the North Hylton Pottery. He was joined in 1813 by Robert Dixon and,

when Phillips died in 1820, William Austin became a partner. Thus the wares of this pottery were marked at various times with the names of all three men. The name 'Garrison' derived from the fact that the pottery was situated next to the Sunderland barracks, with its permanent garrison.

The last important Sunderland manufacturer was the *Wear* or *Moore's Pottery*. It was to become one of the largest on Wearside, producing pink, purple, copper and silver lustre and making a speciality of decorative lustre wall plaques. Marks, incorporating the name of the firm, were usually impressed.

NEWCASTLE UPON TYNE
Most of the Newcastle potteries were clustered along the banks of the Tyne river and will be dealt with in alphabetical order. Nicholas Bird's *Low Lights Pottery* had a very considerable output, even though its products were not generally of the highest quality, even when John Carr took over the business from 1840 onwards.

Robert Maling owned two potteries after

Two moulded pink lustre-decorated jugs with unusual and almost identical handles. The lustre is combined with green enamel backgrounds. Probably from the St Peter's Pottery of Thomas Fell in Newcastle, c.1820-30. Height of larger jug 6½ inches (165 mm).

A very large and striking Newcastle jug, c.1830, decorated in typical Tyneside style and with a transfer print on the side showing the characters William and Susan from an early melodrama. This was Douglas Jerrold's 'Black Ey'd Susan or All On The Downs', which toured England between 1829 and 1860. The picture of the North Shields lifeboat on the front of the jug is after an engraving by Thomas Bewick. Height 9 inches (229 mm).

moving to Newcastle: first the *Ouseburn Bridge*, and then the *Ford Pottery*. The latter was added as the business prospered, until Maling was the largest pottery in the United Kingdom, making, apart from decorated lustred items, a vast range of kitchen ware such as bowls and jelly moulds. The only pottery in the north-east to survive well into the twentieth century, Maling was to produce in the 1920s and later a range of iridescent lustre. The factory finally closed in 1963.

A keen exporter was the *St Anthony's Pottery*, which was acquired by Joseph Sewell about 1804, much of its creamware being made in imitation of that from Wedgwood and finding a ready market on the continent. It began using lustre decoration in 1815 and went on to produce some of the finest and most elegant of Newcastle wares.

A pot-pourri probably from the St Anthony's Pottery of Joseph Sewell in Newcastle, c.1820. The rim is silver lustre on a yellow glazed body. The transfer print is in the style of Bartolozzi. Height 5½ inches (140 mm).

A producer of fine moulded jugs was the *St Peter's Pottery* of Thomas Fell, established in 1817. Its principal output was of white, printed domestic earthenware, but there was also a good deal of lustreware. The mark incorporated the name FELL.

George Patterson's *Sherriff Hill* or *Tyne Pottery* was never a large concern, but it did produce a good deal of lustre of the simple domestic kind, often decorated in the 'cottage' style. The firm had a thriving export market in Norway.

SOUTH WALES

How much lustre-decorated pottery was produced in South Wales is still a matter of debate, but surviving lists of a sale at the Cambrian Pottery's warehouse in London make it clear that lustre was a significant part of Welsh ceramic production. The *Cambrian Pottery* in Swansea began trading in 1794, but it was not until one of its earliest owners, John Dillwyn, took control once more that the main output of pink and purple lustreware began and mugs, jugs, cow-creamers and the plates with perforated borders so much associated with this particular pottery were produced. Some silver and copper lustre work was also carried out. When marked, the wares bore the words CAMBRIAN POTTERY or the single word SWANSEA.

The first of the other two producers of lustreware was the *Glamorgan Pottery*, dating from 1816 as a partnership between

A quintal or finger flower vase of a type made both in Staffordshire and in the north-east, c.1820. The decorative style suggests Newcastle as a possibility, though there is no mark. Height 7½ inches (191 mm).

28

Right: *Pottery cow-creamers or cream jugs were enormously popular, if very unhygienic. The mouth was the spout, the tail the handle, and they were filled from a small hole in the middle of the back. Here, the purple lustre and chestnut spotting is typical of Cambrian Pottery creamers, while the roughly finished green enamelled base is distinctive of Welsh cow-creamers in general. Those from Staffordshire had a more formal base.*

Left: *Impressed with the mark* SWANSEA, *showing a Cambrian Pottery origin, this pastille burner or pot-pourri (because the lid is missing its exact use is uncertain) has a silver-lustre bowl, c.1830. The supporting dolphins are in a deep underglaze blue. Similar pieces were produced by Wedgwood and others. Height 5^1/$_2$ inches (140 mm).*

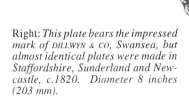

Right: *This plate bears the impressed mark of* DILLWYN & CO, *Swansea, but almost identical plates were made in Staffordshire, Sunderland and Newcastle, c.1820. Diameter 8 inches (203 mm).*

Messrs Baker, Bevan and Irwin and run by Mr Baker. His father-in-law was the manager of the Cambrian Pottery, so that there was a close link between the two and their products were broadly similar. The second manufacturer was the *South Wales Pottery* at Llanelli, dating from 1839. This could be regarded as the successor to the Glamorgan Pottery, taking over its printing plates and absorbing its workers when Glamorgan ceased trading.

OTHER POTTERIES

Very fine silver resist lustreware was produced by the *Leeds Pottery* run by Hartley Greens and Company, who favoured animals and birds in their designs. The *Middlesbrough Pottery*, established in 1831, closely followed the style of decoration set by its neighbours up the coast, Sunderland and Newcastle, and the only other of the Yorkshire Potteries known positively to have produced lustreware was the one at *Ferrybridge*. There is a strong conviction that lustre was also produced by the *Herculaneum Pottery* at Liverpool, though little firm evidence to support it. The same can be said of the *Warrington Pottery*, but there is no doubt about *Bristol* as examples exist bearing not only the name of the pottery but also either the signature or the initials of one of their chief decorators, William Fifield. Pilkington's *Royal Lancastrian Pottery* in Manchester manufactured lustreware in the early twentieth century, ceasing production in 1928.

Finally, in the second half of the nineteenth century some eleven Scottish potteries were to make use of lustre decoration, among them *Alloa*, *Britannia*, *Clyde*, *Glasgow*, *Portobello* and the *Victoria Pottery*. Most favoured the pale yellow iron lustre used to set off stronger enamel colours rather than as part of the main design.

Left: *Three views of a superbly decorated Odd Fellows jug on which has been used a combination of enamel-coloured transfer prints, a pink lustre trim and freehand painting of the floral sprays in both lustre and enamels, c.1820. The transfer print is of Leeds origin so that, though unmarked, the jug probably came from the Leeds Pottery. Height 7 inches (178 mm).*

30

FURTHER READING

This list includes some books that are out of print and obtainable only second-hand or from libraries.

Baker, J. C. *Sunderland Pottery*. Thomas Reed Industrial Press and Tyne and Wear County Council, fifth edition 1984. Covers the lustre output of the Wearside potteries very fully.

Bedford, J. *Old English Lustre Ware*. Cassell, 1965.

Bell, R. C. *Tyneside Pottery*. Studio Vista, 1971.

Bosanko, W. *Collecting Old Lustre Ware*. Heinemann, 1916.

Caiger-Smith, A. *Lustre Pottery*. Faber & Faber, 1985. Concentrates authoritatively on the Hispano-Moresque type of lustre.

Carter, P. *A Dictionary of British Studio Potters*. Scolar Press, 1990.

Cross, A. J. *Pilkington's Royal Lancastrian Pottery*. R. Dennis, 1980.

Des Fontaines, U. *Wedgwood Fairyland Lustre*. Sotheby Parke Bernet, 1975.

Fleming, J. A. *Scottish Pottery*. Mackehose, Jackson & Co, 1923.

Gibson, M., and Godden, G. *Collecting Lustreware*. Barrie & Jenkins, 1991. The only comprehensive, up-to-date book.

Greenwood, M. *The Designs of William de Morgan*. R. Dennis and W. E. Wiltshire, 1989.

John, W. D., and Baker, W. *Old English Lustre Pottery*. The Ceramic Book Company, second edition 1962.

Moore, S., and Ross, C. *Maling, the Trademark of Excellence*. Tyne and Wear Museums Service, 1989.

Nance, E. M. *The Pottery and Porcelain of Swansea and Nantgarw*. Batsford, 1942.

Niblett, P. and K. *Hand-Painted Gray's Pottery*. City Museum and Art Gallery, Stoke-on-Trent, third edition 1987.

A puzzle jug with pink-lustre and enamel decoration from the Bristol Pottery, c.1832. The floral bouquets are very representative of the work of their chief decorator, William Fifield, whose initials appear on the base of the jug. The inscription is interesting but unfortunately not dated. Height 6½ inches (165 mm).

PLACES TO VISIT

The following museums have collections of lustreware but those marked with an asterisk (*) have only a small collection. It should always be borne in mind, however, that whether a collection be large or small it may not always be on display. Reserve collections can sometimes be seen if an appointment is made first, but it is always wise to telephone to find out what is on show before making a long journey to a museum.

*Bantock House Museum**, Bantock Park, Bradmore Road, Wolverhampton, West Midlands WV3 9LQ. Telephone: 0902 312132.

*The British Museum**, Great Russell Street, London WC1B 3DG. Telephone: 071-636 1555.

*Castle Museum**, Norwich, Norfolk NR1 3JU. Telephone: 0603 223624.

Glasgow Art Gallery and Museum, Kelvingrove, Glasgow G3 8AG. Telephone: 041-357 3929.

*Harris Museum and Art Gallery**, Market Square, Preston, Lancashire PR1 2PP. Telephone: 0772 58248.

Laing Art Gallery, Higham Place, Newcastle upon Tyne, Tyne and Wear NE1 8AG. Telephone: 091-232 6989 or 7734.

*Liverpool Museum**, William Brown Street, Liverpool, Merseyside L3 8EN. Telephone: 051-207 0001.

Mansfield Museum and Art Gallery, Leeming Street, Mansfield, Nottinghamshire NG18 1NG. Telephone: 0623 663088.

National Museum of Wales, Cathays Park, Cardiff, South Glamorgan CF1 3NP. Telephone: 0222 397951.

Royal Pavilion Art Gallery and Museum, 4/5 Pavilion Buildings, Brighton, East Sussex BN1 1UE. Telephone: 0273 603005.

Stoke-on-Trent City Museum and Art Gallery, Bethesda Street, Hanley, Stoke-on-Trent, Staffordshire ST1 3DE. Telephone: 0782 202173.

Sunderland Museum and Art Gallery, Borough Road, Sunderland, Tyne and Wear SR1 1PP. Telephone: 091-514 1235.

*Temple Newsam House**, Leeds, West Yorkshire LS15 0AE. Telephone: 0532 641358 or 647321.

*The Victoria and Albert Museum**, Cromwell Road, South Kensington, London SW7 2RL. Telephone: 071-938 8500.

*Warwick District Council Art Gallery and Museum**, Avenue Road, Leamington Spa, Warwickshire CV31 3PP. Telephone: 0926 426559.

Wedgwood Museum, Josiah Wedgwood & Sons Ltd, Barlaston, Stoke-on-Trent, Staffordshire ST12 9ES. Telephone: 0782 204141.

Welsh Folk Museum, St Fagans, Cardiff, South Glamorgan CF5 6XB. Telephone: 0222 596441.